# Logorrhea

**ALSO BY ADRIAN C. LOUIS**

POETRY

*The Indian Cheap Wine Séance*
*Muted War Drums*
*Sweets for the Dancing Bears*
*Fire Water World*
*Among the Dog Eaters*
*Days of Obsidian, Days of Grace*
*Blood Thirsty Savages*
*Vortex of Indian Fevers*
*Ceremonies of the Damned*
*Skull Dance*
*Ancient Acid Flashes Back*
*Bone and Juice*
*Evil Corn*

FICTION

*Skins*
*Wild Indians and Other Creatures*

Adrian C. Louis

# Logorrhea

TRIQUARTERLY BOOKS
NORTHWESTERN UNIVERSITY PRESS
EVANSTON, ILLINOIS

TriQuarterly Books
Northwestern University Press
www.nupress.northwestern.edu



Printed in the United States of America

10 9 8 7 6 5 4 3 2 1

ISBN 0-8101-5177-4 (cloth)
ISBN 0-8101-5178-2 (paper)

**Library of Congress Cataloging-in-Publication Data**

Louis, Adrian C.
Logorrhea / Adrian C. Louis.
p. cm.
ISBN 0-8101-5177-4 (cloth : alk. paper) — ISBN 0-8101-5178-2 (pbk. : alk. paper)
1. Indians of North America—Poetry. 2. United States—Social life and customs—21st century—Poetry. I. Title.
PS3562.O82L64 2006
811.54—dc22 2006015340

The paper used in this publication meets the minimum requirements of the American National Standard for Information Sciences—Permanence of Paper for Printed Library Materials, ANSI Z39.48-1992.

**for Colleen**

*My sky's getting far,*
*the ground's getting close.*
*My self's going crazy*
*the way that it does.*
*I'll lie on my pillow*
*and sleep if I must,*
*too late to wish I'd been stronger.*
TOWNES VAN ZANDT

## Contents

## Acknowledgments

Some poems in this edition, a few in earlier versions, have been published in *Ploughshares, New Letters, Crazyhorse, North American Review, Red Rock Review, TriQuarterly,* and *Nerve Cowboy.* Other poems appeared in the anthology *There Is No Other Way to Speak* (Minnesota Center for Book Arts, 2005) and in the limited edition chapbook *Deer Dreams* (Red Dragonfly Press, 2006).

The author extends special thanks to Susan Betz and her posse at Northwestern University Press. A tip of the old seed cap to Morty Sklar of Spirit That Moves Us Press for the cover and title page artwork by Gay Rogers, which originally appeared in the 1984 book *Nuke-Rebuke: Writers and Artists Against Nuclear Energy and Weapons.* Finally, thanks to Dorianne Laux, Sandy Mosch, and David Pichaske.

# Logorrhea

## An E-mail to Taspan Wi

Just got back to Minnesota. Took the scenic route, Rushville to Gordon, Gordon to Martin, Martin to Mission, Mission to Winner, then north of Winner by Colome. Came upon this Indian guy walking down the road backward, real fast. Freaky. I just kept going, watched him in the rearview mirror. The guy was really covering some ground, but backward . . . Not the kind of hitchhiker you want to pick up. My first thought: *Heyoka.* Immediate second thought was that he was a ghost, which was why I kept going. Third possibility was that he was crazy or half buzzed up and just freaking out oncoming cars. Whatever, it was exquisitely spooky, and he had a goofy smile on his face—not a comical grin, but one of deadly pain.

There is a fourth possibility. It was me, walking fast, walking backward, cussing out every ghost I ever imagined, every ghost that pissed into my ears and danced upon my eyeballs. It was the spirit inside me, kicked outside temporarily to protect me from other truly drooling spirits sent by jealous enemies.

## *Kwe Na'a*

Though blessed sage
bloomed in our ancient valleys,
my generation's beds of birth
and ejaculatory death were
cursed with an eternal confusion
of internal combustion. We enrolled
in tribal demolition derbies and
fell to the fired earth and moaned.
We could not pray, so we crawled
toward the mothering darkness.
We cannot tell you why we spent
a lifetime crawling when we
had wings that were strong,
supremely brown, and so holy.

## Blue Turtle Songs

Late May on a five-mile
stretch of Interstate 90
near Canistota, South Dakota,
dozens and dozens
of turtles marched through
the blood and smashed
flesh of their brothers
upon the blacktop.

For a long and brief
moment I wondered why
these little shellbacks
were crossing the forlorn
road until an ejaculation
of epiphenomenalism clued
me in to the fact that these
little twits were poet turtles.

Of course they were only
trying to get to the other
side but what mattered
more was that they were
driven by the bloodied
memories of their lost
and stolen homelands.

What mattered more than
their destination was
the dark possibility
that they were
on a crying jag

and listening to
blue turtle songs
when their hearts
exploded inside
my soul.

## Rabbit Dance

I'm a squatter here in Jesusland.
One week before the war taxes are due,
engorged winds from Buffalo Ridge
buffet my parked car and snort
boundless detritus past a burgeoning
greenness of lawn where a peculiar
little rabbit huddles and stares at me.
It's only a few feet from the car, so
I lock the beast in an eyeball duel.
It refuses to budge and so do I
as sunshine wraps my '83 Ford
in warmth pungent as an old quilt.
I awaken twenty minutes later
to find the victor has vanished.

⁂

Dear rabbit, I'm snug as a thug
in the cell of my car, procrastinating
a visit to a smug and learned woman
who likes to tickle my tailbone.
Trickster rabbit, this year I've seen
aging friends and allies falter under
the weight of love's corpse and all
I could do was thank the spirits
that I was not them. I've watched
them shake in glittering madness
and substitute logorrhea for logic.
I've seen them rage when kindly
eyes beseeched them for the keys
to their silly love-shorn brains.

Rabbit, brother, do not let me
become one of those quaint,
nervous hobblers. Shit, I've
already staggered down blood
roads as hellish as any man has.
My damn dues are paid in full.
And I have loved one woman
whose loving heart pumped
the contagion of Calvary and
Wounded Knee simultaneously,
and I will love her until I most
miserably die if you, dear rabbit,
will hop back here and convince
me I can live on memories alone,
and if you will then crawl up
into the fan belt and stop
this sad car's engine
from igniting. Rabbit, O
rabbit, I am only asking for
one fortuitous foot, foolish
fetishist that I am.

## Dreaming Bear

Blessed be the weak
and meek, but I'll tumble
grave-way as neither.
There is a woman I have
recently come to know
whose fine young legs I
would slay monsters for,
but then what would
a man in his fifties do
with such fine thighs
were he to win them?
I am boldly stupid to be
still worried at this late
date about finding some
cave for the fat dreaming
bear asleep on my lap.
The medicine man I consult
is not sure if such a thing
is good or bad. He only
shakes his smiling skull,
and I ape him ever so amiably,
drunk on the nectar of possibility.

## Magic Marker Rock Graffiti near Lolo Hot Springs, Montana

Because you . . .
invented your god,
invented your hell,
you are condemned
to each. When I tell
you that I command
certain spirits, then you
really should believe
me when I say that in
this very breath I am
praying for the past
of your future.
—CHIEF JOSEPH

⁂

Great Chief Joseph,
I dance the sweat lodge
dance with you, brother.
Oh, what a true honor
to read your dark words
upon this craggy rock.
I toast you with anything
but white man's woozy water.
I know how those things go
since I had to stage-screw
this alkie Native princess in
*A River Runs Through It.*

(Script said she was Indian,
but then maybe she was
just a little thespian like me.)

—BRAD PITT

※

P.S.
You might not know this,
but I also got mangle-killed
by a Native spirit bear
in *Legends of the Fall.*
Another Montana story . . .
I played Tristan Ludlow,
and in this tall tale I got
to poke another Native.
So you and me, Joseph,
we're damn close to being
blood brothers, bed brothers,
some horseshit like that.

—B. PITT (AGAIN!)

## Pax Americana

Miniaturized and moaning,
invisible vultures fly circles
above your head and flap
wings inches from your ears.
Initially, you feel some unease,
a slight malaise easily shrugged off
until night demons with Kalashnikovs
push past pills to enter your dreams.
You can no longer sleep when
summer makes gates of windows.
You turn your head from shadows
waltzing in corners of your eyes.
Your life is now bereft of all disguise.
All appears as it truly is: pointless,
brief, dark, and deadly. Now might
be a good time to lubricate or return
desert bones to their dry, dark beds.

## At the Minnesota State College in the Winter of My Discontent

Woke up fairly sprightly
on Sunday with only
a very slight hangover
and decided to grade papers.
Made my coffee just right.
Okay, it was Nescafé and tasted
like crap, but liked it . . . I did.
Opened the antique briefcase
from a New England Brooks
Brothers store. It was given
to me in '73 as a bribe for
banging most magnificently.
*Me, old fat half-breed, was*
*once loved by many pretties*
*in panties of the rainbow.*

So I neatly arranged the papers
on the table, savored the Nescafé,
then hurriedly peed and showered.
Dried, I drove to the supermarket
and thought and bought a whole
naked chicken for Sunday dinner.
Then I vacuumed, washed dishes,
and put the plump bird in to bake.
I clipped my toenails. I meditated.
I watched the last half of *Predator*
on TV—one of our favorite flicks.
Then let the chicken cool and made
chicken salad sandwiches—mayo,

onions, thinly sliced celery, finely
chopped pickles, and I don't know
why I chopped the pickles so tiny.
My sandwiches and I migrated
to the well-worn couch and
we watched a "reality" show
on NBC called *Fear Factor.*
Spastic Christ on the cross . . .
Is our nation controlled by
some new and invisible drug
from deepest outer space?
*They were eating dicks on TV.*
All metaphors fizzle and squirt
out the eye's window here. Yes,
they *were* eating parboiled water
buffalo penises—Lord have mercy.
Network TV had schlong gobblers
retching over a filthy 50G prize.

I shuddered, lost interest in food,
switched to CNN, and took
a spasmodic nap and awoke with
a snake of skank slithering from
mouth to mealy brain, so I ate ten
of those mints that sleep in a tin.

Newly minted, I watched *Larry King.*
Brokaw, looking gray and haunted,
babbled about a post-retirement project.
Drank me a tumbler of Teacher's scotch.
Decided to have another. O Teacher's . . .
*Vivat academia, vivant professores.*
*Semper sint in flore!*

One more slug and I was humming
what Peter LaFarge said of Ira Hayes

through the lips of Johnny Cash:
"He won't answer anymore,
not the whiskey-drinkin' Indian,
not the marine that went to war."
Fell asleep deep unto the couch.
Awoke to an IED or RPG nightmare
choreographed by a talking head
saying the war dead in Iraq now
neared twenty-five hundred souls.
Sweet, average American kids
graveyarded for no sane reason.

Monday morning. Woke.
"Monday, Monday," that '60s song,
fruggin' in my scotch-addled head.
Made coffee, *real* Starbuckian beans,
all the while thinking no coffee ever
tasted so good as that of my youth,
boiled thick in a buckaroo percolator,
coffee from a tin can that opened
with a key creating a dangerously
sharp ribbon of shining tin memory,
and at *this* instant, as I caught my
shimmering self in the mirror
of time, I softly sang (a lie):
"We love you, old bastard.
We love you, old gray thing."
I shuddered and winked at myself.

Beyond the dancing strands of tin
I knew the stack of papers waited.
My long-haired brain conjured dire
images of my own faulty education
and how a poor boy transported to
an Ivy League institution learned
to disabuse middle-class values,

learned how America was built
upon the broken backs of too
many million nonwhite men.
I shook my head and did what
needed to be done. I got in
my farty old car and went
to the store for supplies.
I thought about driving
to Sioux Falls to get
my ashes hauled but
decided against it.
It was going to be
a damn long winter.

# The Carcinoma Cowboy

*Oh, a false clock tries to tick out my time*
*to disgrace, distract, and bother me.*
BOB DYLAN

## I

When wild white hairs
sprouted out of my ears,
most lies to myself slowed,
though I still cannot disarm
that seemingly alien voice
which forces me to write
endless embellished obituaries
before that tired tire of my
soul is softly deflated.

That voice tells me that
I'd like to think at least
*some* of my foolish footsteps
will be forever frozen in
the cold mud of history.
It demands that one or
a handful of others recall
the sublime insignificance of
my necessary tales of dark
things bumping in the white
night of my slow dying.
That voice announces that
while I yet live, I might like
a drunken brawl of a wake
for the demise of desire.

It's been too many years since
I was rode hard—put away wet.
So in my gray slowing life I
must defer to that voice. Last
spring when a wild young mare
cantered into my corral, I nodded
as if she were just another ghost.
When she trotted up and said,
"I am a horse too," I truly knew
she was only going to play me.
And she knew that I knew.
Thus, the game commenced.
"What have you seen?" I asked.
"Not as much as you, master."
Okay, it's not like I expected.
*Yes sir, yes sir, three bags full.*
"But you *do* know things," I said.
"That I truly do, sire." *Sire . . .*
It was going to be easy to let
her kill me. My anticipation
was appallingly salacious, so
when she did the quick dance
with her scalpel, all that bled
was her deliciously evil smile.
Perhaps a valuable lesson, I
told my still breathing self.
*There is no fool like an old fool*
*whose blue dreams fail to note*
*that nothing is as beautiful as*
*an ordered universe where he*
*can look forward to a measured*
*mouthful of heavenly dirt.*
But then she only opened me
up, rearranged me, left me to
slog through more syrupy time.

I clicked my sticky boot heels
three times and whispered,
"There's no fool like an old fool."

**II**

Oh, a false cock tried to crow
out my days and dismay,
disfigure, and bugger me.
And the dirt of gossip
grew on my face,
and the ghost dust
of tumors covered me.
But if the marrow was great
and the cells were not sick,
they could pierce through
lust no matter how thick.
So I greased up my hand
and remained where I sat
and said adios like
I gave a rat's ass.

**III**

She cut me deep and hard, and for
weeks I moaned with pedophile
priests loitering at my bedside.
A tireless sun mooned no backside.
Only the sweet slot machine drop
of morphine drip soothed the ragged
sutures of middle age and painted
a peculiar hell upon my slow eyes.
I stood at the trembling crossroads
where drugs end—psychosis begins.
At least the priests had scurried away,
and through windows washed daily, I
saw an ordered world. No immaculate
conception of weeds unto sidewalks.

No broken beer bottles sparkled on
the pavement of this Plains city.
The streets were freshly washed.
In the ordered living rooms
of newly painted small houses
every single television pimped
the sparkly, minted smiles
of sweet-speaking skulls.
Serene parents, knee-bouncing
cherubim, gasped glossolalia
at their mind control machines.

All was a perfect lie and I saw
the immaculate sham of evangelism.
I sensed the perfection of demons
rising from the Shroud of Turin.
The essential chaos of the universe
was cloaked, ordered, and humbled.
In a thick morphine haze, I heard
the very soul being sucked out
of surrounding saline prairies.
In the itchy embrace of a hospital
bed, I realized we'd be better
off as clean, hairless meat
for gray off-world carnivores
who like their choice cuts lean.
Dizzy, I fled the surgical ward
AMA and drove by sanitized
Rapid Creek, where Skin winos
with shined shoes, tart smiles,
and pressed white shirts strolled
by, twirling their bumbershoots.
In the piss-yellow light of dawn,
a fey April wind found no single
piece of trash to kiss and blow.

And on every other corner, black
SUVs held suited men with ashen
skin and Ray Charles sunglasses.
MP3s stroked their ears as they
cradled MP5 submachine guns.
These obedient public servants
were garbage collectors, waiting
for anyone to breathe truth,
waiting to thin the feral herd
placidly grazing in Badlands
surrounding this shiny hill city.
They were waiting for me too,
but they'd have to wait longer.
A pulsing roan mare was waiting,
an eagle feather tied to her mane.

## *Tomaano*

There was crusted snow on
the dry slopes of my loins
until my sixteenth spring
when my tongue became
a wild springtime river
with *cui-ui* dancing away
from this desert the white
savages had stolen under
the rubric of Jesus Christ.
I took up the pen like I
would later take up the jug
and wrote skewed history
like today's entry, forty-two
long winters after the first:

*Garter-held nylons wrap*
*young brown thighs that*
*predate glum Golgotha*
*by twenty thousand years,*
*and for those very thighs*
*a continent of feathered felons*
*will attack wagon trains, the Internet,*
*their very own culture, whatever,*
*whomever, when a bartender's*
*bugle sounds the last call.*

## A Small Drama Unfolds Ten Miles South of Kadoka, South Dakota

I pull off the old road
and loiter in tall, dry grass
stretching my creaky back
when I spot the still beast
bleeding in the ditch.
A few fat, nasty flies are
skating on the frozen eyes
of the newly dead deer.

Creators of carrion come.
Clad in pimp orange, pale
huffing humanoids close
the semiarid ground
between the sacred
and the profane.

I wince and wish
I had a Glock, anything to
properly oxygenate them,
but all I do is whip out my
raison d'être and demonstrate
a wet and probable cause for
standing alone on parched
Badlands where life was
once taken with honor,
with humble, starving love.

## Deer People near Platte, South Dakota

They stand on their tiptoes
taking newly minted leaves
from low-hanging branches.
I'm only fifteen feet away
and I know they know
I'm leering at them.
My car window is open
to vent the cigarette smoke.
*Hey, my relatives,* I whisper.
Their ears twitch and stiffen.
They give me a scornful look
and continue green munching.

*Oh, my sweet darlings,*
*when and why did I stray*
*from the loving herd? How*
*did I become this impotent*
*creature with three weak legs?*

## April in Oglala

Here where I have driven
past a thousand times,
here off the two-lane
blacktop, the tattered
blanket of April tries
to warm the icy lies
and whys of what lies
a few feet beneath
the surface of what we know.
A loud yellow backhoe
and several diggers delve
into the hardened breasts
of our Mother Earth
and extract a spirit.
The spirit smiles briefly
at the mix of sun and sadness.
Somewhere someone sings:
*In the sweet by and by,*
*We shall meet on that beautiful shore.*
One spirit is going home, away
from this dark, violent red land.

*for Martín Espada*

## Talking to Jesus the Bug, the Last of His Race, I Think

*And I believe God is great, all praise due to him.*
*And if I should die, I'll rise up to the sky*
*Just like Jesus, peace be upon him.*
STEVE EARLE

In the beginning there was a slew
of them, but I'm down to one
box elder bug tonight and I'm
treating it like a pet since my sweet
dogs departed some three years ago.
It's been below zero all week long.
Last night two bugs were on my desk.
In the morning one had drowned in
the dregs of my wineglass, so tonight
only one dances under dim lamplight,
rubbing his legs like some filthy fly.
Perhaps he's giving me the evil eye,
but I love him like the Lord Jesus.
I go to the fridge, take out a small
twig of celery, run water over it,
and drop it beneath the lamp.
I await the genie or Jesus.
Genie of the stiffest stiffy.
Jesus of the fishy fingers.
Genie of the lesser years.
Jesus of the wilderness.
Genie of the sharp brain.
Jesus of the thorn pain.
Genie of the loving death.
Jesus of the sacred breath.
Jesus of the fearful death.

The little critter just loves
the lamp but wants no celery.
I flick him onto the vegetable.
He runs back to the lamp.
This may be the last supper
I ever offer the little ingrate.
Before the night is over
I just might betray this ray
of light who is my Lord.

⁂

Day two and we are still alive.
Night has fallen somewhere and
Jesus the bug is on his back flailing.
*Help, I've fallen and I can't get up.*
*Help, I've aged and can't get it up.*
I take the tip of my pen and set him
upright. The Lord doesn't even
doff his halo and I suppose I
should be thankful for that.

⁂

Day three, nine at night.
Jesus has found his disciples.
I don't know where his twelve
evangelical homeboys came
from, but they're preaching to
every single object on my desk.
My unused pens do not really
like being talked down to, but
tolerance is the name of the game
until—until one of the little fops
goes skinny-dipping in my red
sea of cheap Australian Shiraz.

Then I get the vacuum and suck
them down, darkly down, one
by Jerusalem one, deep into
the eternal shudder and
sheer fiction of biblical hell.

Then, only then, there is peace
in the valley, and tonight God
is good, God is great. All
praise due to him.

## Logorrhea

Big city scares. Older I get.
Hey, Murderapolis, Minnesota, too
much shit going down, walk,
don't run, politicians say, but
too much scum is escaping
the reaper here, this fecal burg.
Too many car chases, hairy meth
bitches killing. Baldy gang bitches
killing. Cop bitches killing and
me scurrying from car to store
wishing I could redact "olly olly
oxen free" and quit hiding from
my fear of man, just tether my ass
like an ancient Cheyenne dog soldier
or, better, bare my throat as a young
weak wolf would, but I can't do either—
why the hell should I?—too bad I can't
kill, just kill the bastards with words.
Line the murderers up and watch
them crumple on the lonely prairie.
Make them pray to any ancient god.
His low thunder after the distant fact
of lightning from a Sharps Buffalo Rifle.
God nasty, the cleansing lightning.
God explosive, the erotic rain of blood.

## *Toh Gah Kwa*

It took me a half century
to appreciate the circularity,
the sacred hoop connection,
of tail to mouth in the one-
eyed monster that refused
to blind me to the dirt ways
of the soiled and broken.
I was only a common man.

I was only a common man.
I always sought out, relished,
shattered Skins who babbled
and hobbled down any filthy
and acrid street of despair.
When I danced with them,
I savored our wild scent,
the cacophonous stink rising
from the profound yet pitiful
sex flower we named survival.
It was no night-blooming cereus.
It was only them, me, just us.
Just us, and it was sweet as hell.

## To the Green Dominatrix Wading in the Wake of 9/11

I stand before her, fat and free,
so smug in my slovenly ways.
I eye her whip with loutish glee,
but she says to lower my gaze.
My humble eyes fall to her boots
when she orders me to my knees.
I utter a prayer for all us brutes
who so foolishly do as we please.
She chains me in a dungeon deep
and sharp with symmetrical rock.
I cry black tears in blacker sleep.
She says she's cutting my cock!

*I think those were the words she used*
*to infuse my chaos with true direction.*
*Confined to strictures, I'm now confused*
*how to conclude with no pen of erection.*

## Baby Blue

No, not a hell of a lot in your eyes
today, *winyan,* some tiny dancers
deep in the corners, miniaturized
shadow people grouping,
soon to chorus: *All the love*
*we ever had is gone . . .*
The well-worn path to all we knew
is overgrown, damn mad with weeds.
Oh, those years of stoned dancing
to ancient anthems whispering now:
*All the love we ever had is gone.*
So when we're dutifully dead, darling,
the ghosts of my clichés will haunt
dark basements of doomed libraries.
There, where the last squirts of lost
poets dry inside forgotten stacks of
imprisoned history, some searcher
might open the mildewed pages
of a book, maybe this very book,
and then our old world will
shimmer and we'll shyly kiss,
desperadoes in the synapses
of some pale stranger's mind.

## Electronic Epistle, or Apology to a Lady in the Bitterroots

The Szechuan beef takeout
from the supermarket deli
tonight was quite suicidal.
Tired, tough-ass vegetables
terrorized my old choppers.
The meat was hot, erotically
spiced, but had the texture
of ancient elm bark—could
have been cat for all I know.
I wish I had the balls to take
the crap back, ask for a refund,
but I can't—Louisiana's gone
mad, helicopters are plucking up
shrieking poor people like turds
floating in cesspool New Orleans.
Federal response from FEMA has
been an unmitigated clusterfuck.
A five-day maelstrom of looters
dancing atop corpses floating
down stinking stagnant streets
made sleazoid cops run away.
Maybe it wouldn't be so damn
horrific if I'd had a decent meal.
I wish I could divorce my TV
because the damn commercials
are so increasingly populated
with today's necessary palette
of young, beautiful people
who are obviously put there
by ugly witches who stink

no matter how much perfume
they swim in, dire creatures
whose fat, hooked noses
are immune to the stench
of their own sordid history.
I despise these witches
and would truly hate them
and their mindless ways if
I didn't feel pity for them too.
I know it's crazy to pity those
whose religion is greed and I
instruct my students to avoid
such a path though I'm paid by
the pound for my own sad soul.
My whiskey voice says to love
my enemies, and for chrissakes,
I do, I really do, the bastards,
but I'm in dire need of meat 'n'
potatoes and your brown skin
and I'm sorry because I know
you have no patience at all
for the yellow-robed choir
inside my inebriated TV
singing ever so softly:
*Shall we gather at the liver,*
*the beautiful, the beautiful liver?*

## Bitterroot Lady Again

I hereby order you
to be naughty tonight.
When the jaundiced moon
makes skeletons of ponderosa,
undo your long black braids.
I'll be there soon, my newest love.
When the crazed owl blurts
its treacherous song, know
that it sings not for us.
Let the buckskin slide off
your shimmering skin
and let our red sin begin
with or without me.

## An Archaic Photo: Two Views

**I**

I have not seen that old
me in many moons and I do
look excruciatingly young, dark
summer brown, and deliciously
tempting for the gray shark I am
now nibbling on the ancient yet
immature flesh in this photo.

In the puffy and bleeding palm
of my chronic hand I cradle
the verifiable essence of
the ignorance of youth.
*But who was that foolish kid*
*and what kind of spaceship*
*fuel was he running on*
*thirty-odd years ago?*

**II**

Those were comfortable
boots once broken in,
top-of-the-line shiny
black Tony Lamas, but
my shit-kicking days
are gone, long gone.
*Oh God, I had taps on them . . .*
And I don't mean to offend
my own ghost, but this photo
needs less profane propane.

I could say it has nothing or
I could say it has too much,
that it needs no cheap booze
pissed into its corners because
it already reeks of full moons,
the poverty of sad woodstoves
raising quaint and dire vapors
like stakes into any weak
future's fluttering heart.
I could say that, I guess,
but what's done is done
and I still worship demons
I once wished to crucify.

*Como era en el principio,*
*ahora y siempre, por los*
*siglos de los siglos. Amén.*

## The Triggering Town

Unscripted yet so dramatic,
a ghost and his self-puncture
of heart by blade is done in
the name of fright, but all my
ghosts have lost their scare.
"*Por favor,* let me lick blood,"
I say half in a faux-agrarian
stupor and half in a romantic,
academic vampirism one
adopts at a cow college.

Quite unperturbed, another
ghost blurts, "Take that stupid
knife out of your drone gland."
A third ghost, the tender one
of the small flock, says, "Yes,
but don't stitch it up, it has
to heal from the inside out."
*At least someone speaks poetry.*

I lower the level of the single
malt jug on the kitchen table,
and I'm starting to levitate,
still medicating the wounds
of a sad red soul first tended
almost four decades ago. But
my wounds have long turned
to scars, so any fiery ablution
is cosmetic or, worse, theatric.

Seeing the ghost's heart paint
red the drunken folly around
us, I recall a noted poet smirking
and sober when I slurred scorn
at him some thirty years ago.

*Young, drunk, and foolish,*
*I chided him for forsaking*
*the sacred sauce of Satan and*
*he died not long after and now*
*I'm as old as that Missoula poet*
*ever was and death-head moths*
*are banging against the windows*
*of the shack I've become.*

"Brothers, let me drink your pain."
Such tremolo with no drum is
a false honor song for red ghosts
and the ever-recurring demise
of our ridiculous sobriety.
The spirits at the worn table
look at me and shrug, knowing
that I will never stop looking
for approval and for fresh,
thick blood to slurp while I
groin-bump into the inevitable.

## Dances with Sheep

MEMORANDUM: REGARDING WINE AND CHEESE RECEPTIONS

We must allow some sheep (*despite any and all infantile and essentially anal-retentive protestations from the Canis Resources Office re the corruption of youth, whatever . . .*) at our moonlight receptions because we wolves will only howl of hemorrhoids if no new blood is present. Our pack must develop friendships with the sheep because there are surely few to be found within the granite glands of our insipid colleagues. And just because one might have sex with a sheep doesn't mean one has to listen to anything uttered—God forbid. Should they babble, merely grab their ears and pull them down toward the nether regions. Pretend, if you must, that you're gathering wool. Oh, comrades, sheep, after all, are not all that bright, are they? And if they are, how did it become so?

## The Hurdy-Gurdy Man

I'm mired deep in the beast,
breathless in the born-again
ass air of Marshall, Minnesota.
On the couch of middle age, my
cabled machine of thoughtlessness
glows me unto forests of Indonesia
being cleared for pulp mills which
make paper for computer printers,
for *my* computer printer, for the
very page of this feeble scrawl.

Had I a larger crayon I might ask
where America's conscience is.
I might expand, ask how we've
allowed mindless bloodsuckers to
steer our ship and why it is these
captains of industry won't admit
the crazy weather is an omen of
our eventual death. I do admit
that I've spent a lifetime asking
such dire and gloomy questions,
all the while understanding quite
clearly the very nature of our nation.
Comrades, in this testimony I can
only say that I sometimes follow
and film myself, though I barely
know how to turn on a computer
in my cell-sized factory office.
Not totally stupid, I surely know
our current American regime is
as dark as any our sad history

has ever conjured, which makes
it all the more tragic that in
the name of "homeland security"
I must say one late night last
week I drove by my house
intending to visit, have a few free
shots, when I witnessed my naked
silhouette dancing in a manner
most aboriginal to an ancient,
soul-soothing Donovan album
spinning serenely at 33 and 1/3,
and instead of stopping,
I sped away in fear.

*The peep show I provided*
*frightened me much more*
*than any potential destruction*
*of this dry world's rain forests,*
*so I had no choice but to*
*inform the effing FBI*
*of this terror in my heartland.*

## Milking the Venom

Rank and tenure don't trump
ridiculous temptations born
of the bare midriffs and visible
thongs of the current coed style.
I should be glad I'm not young
again, I tell myself, and laugh
away the frantic drums
of tachycardia prompted
by tattoos above the perfect
butt cracks of small-town girls.

And I cannot be offended by
sideways-cap-wearing boys
who can't conjugate any verb
except the infinitive "to drink."
Lord, there's little else to do
at a Division II factory except
seek ways to become invisible
to boredom, which may be why
earlier today I decided to file
my fingernails in the sanctuary
of the parking lot and listen to
Don Imus bitching on the radio
and thus missed a subcommittee
of a subcommittee meeting.
I hereby freely admit that I
may be a "disgruntled employee,"
but I also realize in any state
institution that is the term for
one whose eyes trick his tongue
into babbling the simple truths.

I *am* my own brother-in-arms.
I could give more disgruntled
grunts but none of this really
matters because I accept the
dire shadows my age imposes.
I am a professor of slugology
at old Slug State University.
*Oh, yes, you know what I mean.*
Too many of *you* have learned to
slide down *your* own slimy paths
with only the faintest though clearly
amoral amount of spurt and spittle.

"Slugs," I whispered in afterthought.
"Slugs," I echo-whispered back.
It could be worse, but I've learned
to become invisible to Machiavellian
dilettantes, faux radical Satanistas,
and bloodsucking Oompa-Loompas
of the painfully ordinary variety.
Radiant, I rose from my car cave
meditation with enough venom
milked to totter toward spring
break, salvation, all other
illusions of sanity.

## In the Factory of the Mind

In an aerie of Sturm and Dreck,
the pervasive drone dominating
our factory is not the squeal
of the dynamos but the united
and victorious moan of
its very namesake, those
*forever* newly minted, those
supercilious suck-ass drones.

In the sarcastic, brilliant futility
of backbiting, the dynamos,
those bright and snarky
queens of honey-brained
kisses, killed their kin
and cut off invisible
stingers to spite their faces.

Decloaked like a Klingon
Bird-of-Prey, this demise
of the dynamos did not birth
even one ironic "fare-thee-well"
like MacArthur's "Old soldiers
never die, they just fade away."
We were oh-so-dutifully dead,
but let history record that in
the lightness of our peculiar
moments, we armored queens
dogfought and spun earthward,
wounded and dying but still as
haughty as well-bred whores.

With a quick genuflection unto
the very vacuum of default,
the evil-dull drones took over.
Now, bland cheerleaders with pink
pom-poms of amoral crepe parade
throughout our factory screeching
and drooling, "We drones have won,
all hail us, you guys—come on now.
*All* hail us damnable drones."

So we bow down and await
the next end of the next world,
the next universe, the next university.

## The Arrow Bar in Sioux Falls

Temporarily averse to any factual
detailing of the actual, I will only
admit that in the almighty *then*
of a dark space-time continuum
I was nursing a Pepsi in the Arrow
Bar in Sioux Falls (yes, I know)
when this pale drunk piped up
and said he was a Mixedblood.

He was Cherokee-Irish Métis
and no damn half-breed Indian.
This dude was a Mixedblood. His
capital *M* signified a new nation.

*Imprimis was the Mixedblood.*
*The brother was representing.*

I'd heard such portraits before,
so I simply shrugged and tried
to gum some stale pretzels.
I had my choppers hidden
in a T-shirt pocket—I mean,
I wasn't there to snag, I was
just minding my own business,
soaking in a sea of red I had
not splashed in for a while.

I floated silently, but questions
popped like corn from the mouth
of a bedraggled transvestite

from Upper Cutmeat sitting
two seats down and dirty.

She began grilling the white meat:
You grow up around any Skins?
        *No.*
So are you an enrolled member
of a federally recognized tribe?
        *No.*
Any your relatives got brown skin?
        *What kind of question's*
        *that, for Christ's sake?*
Ever took welfare? Sold blood?
        *What's your point?*
Have you ever punched someone
just 'cause your knuckles itched?
        *No.*
You like to kiss me now or later?
        *Not now, not later,*
        *you're ridiculous,*
        *and besides I'm*
        *a member of AIM.*
        *I walked point in 'Nam.*
        *White boys called me Chief.*

Chief Sitting Bullshit, she said.
This Sicangu girl was relentless.
This Skin was getting under
the foreskin of the non-Skin.
But the guy just didn't get it
since she was being ridiculous
in a rowdy, ridiculous rez way.

I watched her snarf down draft
after draft, and then when I
turned my eyes to the tube to
see a moonwalking pedophile
stroll into court in his jammies,
I heard her rez fist mash hard
against his Mixedblood nose.
His mixed blood flowed
as he fled out the door
and one small Sioux girl
had won one small war.
So I put in my teeth, sucked
in my gut, and ordered a beer
to honor her brave heart, but
then dancing red spiders
flashed in from the street
and brutal-bored Bluecoats
hauled her queer rear away.

## Reunion Dance

Sun kissed snow.
River licked sand.
I swam like *Cui-ui,*
and the shit of winter
washed from my ass.
I danced into you
like the sweet spring
sage rising from our
dry desert earth.

*My high school love,*
*our dry earth was*
*once misted with*
*the young and foolish*
*dreams of the two parched*
*strangers we would fight*
*lifetimes against becoming.*

## The Dark Resurrection of the Son of Worm and Attendant Apocrypha

*Things aren't quite the same when I'm rushing*
*on my run and I feel just like Jesus' son . . .*
LOU REED

*He tried to recall if the white holy men had ever spoken of how their Christ defined himself after he was reborn.* First, he remembered his ancient self and the pain from a bayonet raping his kidney. But he remembered the youthful days of his second self, his reborn self, even stronger. One day he's eighteen and the Jaynetts are injecting "Sally go round the roses / Roses, they can't hurt you," and he's bouncing around on a stiff pecker, and then the next day he's in his fifties and needs the jack of black tar to get off the pavement. Even though he's doing the only job he ever wanted, there comes the day when he realizes the best view of Minnesota might be in the rearview mirror. He does not know how much longer he can drive to work down the ice roads of ball-biting winter with a searing ghost woman in the cage of his head. Even though he still has the strong medicine of a round stone tied to his ear, one ghost won't let him be. Weeks earlier, angel wings had started to beat about an inch from his earlobes. That was okay. All the high-frequency voices he heard (he was sure they weren't his) were most likely those of ally spirits, and he could live with that. It was not like his teeth fillings were tuned into the singing instructions of deep-space aliens or Son of Sam voices offering bad advice and other clues to textbook schizophrenia. The spirits sang to him, and that was acceptable to his primitive heart. It was his *own* singing with his chin thrusting and head bobbing that bothered him more.

His singing (if you could call it that) was far beyond the Psych 101 of dumb-fat Dr. Phil on dumb-fatter Oprah and far beyond his thin keening in any imagined *inipi.*

He wasn't exactly sure when his chin music began, but it was some weeks before Xmas. It erupted sporadically and initially was easily repressed, but then it became uncontrollable. Now, every morning for the past month, approaching the factory through the haze of the corn-manufacturing plant in the low-slung industrial park, he sang, "Oh, bang me in the big butt, my little pig butt frozen pizza town." He knew not what it meant, but he sang loudly, a basso profundo reverberating like woofers in the Camaros of the local high school cretins, a deep moaning throb darker than Paul Robeson's rendition of "Old Man River." In the rare sneezes of clarity that the sane claim as their constant province, he regarded the song as a perverse gaudeamus igitur, and because it never failed to arouse some deep cretinous dance within his trembling brain, he forced himself to sing it in bemused contentment. "Oh, bang me in the big butt, my little pig butt frozen pizza town." It was an act of dissolution, an act of contrition, and a proud anthem of sedition. It was a song devised to insert itself in the posterior of the sad Jesusland he found his body now roaming. *Anoint me now, Lord, forever in-a-gadda-da-vida.*

⁕

The perfectly plump Nepali girl is wearing skintight denim slacks with bleached stitches. Not a good sight for the middle-aged horndog. The white stitches run exactly along the crack of her vibrant ass. No, not good at all, *papa-oom-mau-mau.* He goes outside in the minus-twenty gloom and smokes a smoke. For once there is no howling Buffalo Ridge wind. He notices some white hairs on his thin black coat and brushes them off. Hoary hairs. White as the frozen tears he has stored in his frigid heart from his failed dreams of love. Nothing to say but "Oh." Oh. Think of the saddest love song you ever heard and compound it with the pain of a rusty mousetrap snapping unto your privates. That is exactly the mad, hopping dance of love that besets him from time to time. Think of the tears of guilt one faces upon the death of a hated loved one. *Father, can you help an old altar boy? I'm a Catholic.*

Oh, if he were a studly stud from a high-caste Nepali family, he might saunter up to the ravishing beauty and say, "Katmandu kitten, what up?" He grinds the stub of the Marlboro between the packed snow and his Kmart shoes. He shakes his head at the visualization of his fifty-four-year-old Oscar Mayer, inept and flaccid, intruding upon the foreign fiction of eighteen-year-old Himalayan flesh. He knows he is a fool and any redemptive action is folly at his age, but what kind of an option is death? When he slogs back inside, the Nepali girl is standing outside the department office reading the bulletin board. "Oh, bang me in the big butt, my little pig butt frozen pizza town," he hums ever so quietly. He thinks she's been hanging around the office for three days in a row, saying a shy hello to him, but then maybe it's only been one time and two lustful mirages. Okay, it becomes obvious what he must do. When the angel of death knocks at your door, you offer what you have: *Please, sir, come in. Would you have a Budweiser and a fried-egg sandwich? The power of Christ compels you. The power of Christ compels you.* He would have to tie her up and lick her toes until she confessed she was a redskin in disguise. "Oh, Black Buffalo Woman, I knew you were you. Let us break-dance then upon the road of ghosts."

⁂

It was a sad tale that skated inexorably upon his frozen eyes. One fine day he decided he simply could not carry out the sham of the American dream anymore, so he stabbed it repeatedly with the bayonet of a blue icicle. Putrid bile escaped from its wounds and it sagged like a deflated balloon and died. Or so he thought until the reborn and still-bleak fixation reentered his sad-shadowed brain the following day when the alarm clock rang. He tried to recall where he placed his well-worn copy of *De Exorcismis et Supplicationibus Quibusdam.*

The sky is bleak and heartless. He has fallen completely out of disguise. There is a ravishing Lakota girl sitting at his kitchen table. He is in an adjoining room at his desk looking for some way to impress her. For a moment the dark Indian face of his grandmother on the wall distracts him. What does he say to a cliché deferred? *Grandmother on the wall—he is older than you when you died. And he now confesses that he'll have no grandson to put his picture on a wall. Christ, you knew the pain of the excruciatingly ambivalent.* Once, somewhere over the ancient Badlands, he watched the Blue Angels go from a tight formation and explode into a crazed starburst. *Young bright white boys in the sky with no fear of death—how could his feathered ancestors comprehend?* Of course, a starburst of dissolution is what happened to his family. It is what happened to all those he loved. It is what has happened to his own brain since he grew older than his grandmother in the trauma of rebirth. Starburst. Brain burst. Logorrhea shaded solidly by the never-ending need for love. The bleak and sorrowful hunger for love, for dreams of love if nothing else. And words, crazed words. Logorrhea. A confused starburst of nouns and verbs producing only a Lakota girl's ghost, waiting for his wordless, anxious, and ravenous tongue. Must always the snake slide into Eden? *Oh, bang me in the big butt, my little pig butt frozen pizza town.*

⁂

He dreams in blue of Black Buffalo Woman. The dream unravels in a second-story room of a Victorian house, not a true Victorian like one would see in New England but one suitable enough (he guesses) for the pitiful Twin Cities, the last refuge of liberalism. The high ceilings are covered with white-painted tin and plaster. Something about the house whispers of Itchycoo Park. He is at a mahogany desk drawing glyphs and squiggles on tanned doeskin. Finished, he calls out to her to come and interpret what he's drawn. What gives him the authority to demand her presence he does not know. He points from symbol to symbol, and she says she does know what they mean but wonders why he should be drawing such texts. She leans in closer to him, too close, and he points to some miniaturized characters he has squiggled. "That's my name," she says. Apparently he can write in symbols. "And those characters underneath your name? Do you know what that says?" "It says death will dance close again, very close," she whispers.

Some seconds or centuries later, she bends even closer and the blue silk blouse she is wearing brushes his face. He turns his blue head, opens his mouth to her breast, and grips her brown nipple gently with his dry lips. Obediently, she backs away and starts to take off her blouse. "Wait," he says and gets up and walks down the hall to a bathroom where the shower is running and irritating him immensely. "Who the hell left this petulant thing on?" he murmurs. He thinks of taking a shower, knows he should probably launder his fat penis, but turns the water off instead. Then he saunters back to the room she was in, but she's vanished. He bolts to the window and peers outside. Something blue is on the lawn. It's her. She is squatting on the lawn two stories down. There's a tall aluminum ladder leading down to the ground. Quickly, he goes out the window and down the ladder and helps her to her feet. He asks first if she is real and then if she is okay. She says yes-yes, and then out of nowhere her husband is at her side. *Her husband?* He supposes that somewhere in the recesses of his aging mind he knew she had a husband, that his name is No Water. Why is it in both lives he fell in love with women who were totally unavailable? *Why did destruction often have a delicious taste?* This man, her husband, was obviously *akicita.* Well, what should he be? It's not like she'd be married to some forlorn Lutheran farmer or something. They both help her to the ladder and then up it, climbing back toward the window to her room. Halfway up, they stop. Her husband is ahead of her, holding her hand. The hero of this tale is below, making sure Black Buffalo Woman and No Water don't tumble down. And he damn sure has the better view. Black Buffalo Woman is wearing blue panties. Looking up, he sees them stop because she says she is out of breath and can't go on. Then her husband reaches into his pocket and hands her a lump of dark substance. She puts it in a small pipe and smokes it. "What poison is she taking?" he asks. The husband answers lamely that it is *pejuta* and that she has been taking it for many moons. Upset by the cliché of such news, he dashes up the ladder toward the couple, grabs hold of her braid, and says, "I won't let you go back into the room unless you promise to quit killing your soul." She looks at him with wordless blue tears in her eyes. If he took a hundred sad love clichés and squeezed them like a sponge and drank the bitter liquor, he could still not taste the true eternal sadness of turquoise tears. Her bitter tears dance toward his blue-red heart, and all he can think of is suckling her brown breasts, of being her ancient child. "You give me all that evil shit," he says to her husband. "Okay," says the husband, "but you first gotta give up any claims to the spirits of the past, you twice-dead dickhead."

⁂

Somewhere between the death of love and the love of death, he tries to figure out exactly where he is and where he has been. Halfway between high plains dusk and duty, a passing state trooper gives him the evil eye, pulls him over, and tells him to put on the seat belt. The trooper resembles the old actor Lee Marvin, so he immediately clamps on the seat belt, which he hates. On the way home from Sioux Falls, where he's had his horns trimmed by a buckskin girl, and a dozen mile markers past the Minnesota state line, he almost takes the seat belt back off again. Screw Lee Marvin. He recalls an old war movie, maybe *The Big Red One* or maybe *The Dirty Dozen,* but there's this pregnant Frenchwoman stretched out like some naked *maja* about to give birth. The GIs try to help her and Marvin asks how to say "push" in French. "Pooh-say," one of the soldiers says. So Marvin says, "Pooh-say, pooh-say" to the prone woman. He's staring straight at her and finally he lets slip "Puh-see." And this said with the straightest of faces. Hooray for Hollywood . . . *Father, can you help an old altar boy? I'm a Catholic.*

He's riding the black tar and eating KFC, it's not like his arteries could be harmed any more than they already have been. He chomps on a breast, gets a small bone stuck in his throat, and panics. How does one Heimlich oneself? He takes both hands off the steering wheel and speeds past the rumble strip and onto the soft shoulder. He freaks further and hits the brakes and skitters down into a ditch and flips the car. Thank God the seat belt has him hog-tied. Spun head over heels, all he can think of is that one time after football practice when he and three close Skin friends went over to the bleachers where the blond cheerleaders were practicing and they imitated them doing cartwheels, these jocks still in their cleats and shoulder pads. They swore they could smell the wetness beneath the surface scorn of the white girls. So be it. In the freezing now of Now, he has flipped cartwheels in his battered '83 Crown Vic, and things go black, bleaker than the starless Great Plains night. When he comes to, he hears voices talking Indian, men and women, dogs, kids, and horses on the move. He peers out the window and sees his upside-down people dressed in the old way and moving to fresher land. The car is sitting on its roof, and the people march by without even a glance, except for one old woman. She wears a long shawl made of rabbit skins and smiles a toothless grin when her eyes meet his. "Black Buffalo Woman, help me," he says in his own Indian language. Though hardly enthusiastic, she seems to understand. She shuffles up to the car, reaches her ancient hand through the shattered driver's side window, and pushes the button on the seat belt. He crashes down onto the roof of the car. He untangles himself and crawls out the window. He staggers, stares, and sees no one. Not one red soul. The ancient migrating redskins have vanished. He throws up and sits down and closes his eyes. One would think the mind would produce more spinning chaos, but for some reason at that very instant he swallows the banal image of silent, snowy fields.

He was canned in his old Crown Victoria halfway down a forty-foot drop-off, and he knows he's lucky to be out and alive. He could be dead twice, first from going off the road and rolling the car, and second from choking to death on a chicken bone. Fate wedged in his throat, simple as that, and he panicked. He tried to pull onto the shoulder but hit some snow and down into the ditch he went. He screamed as he left the road, and Christ almighty that's when the chicken bone jumped out of his throat. *Still, better to be killed a second time by greasy Colonel Sanders in the doom between high plains dusk and dark than his first death in the stockade in the Nebraska panhandle by his* kola *Little Big Man.*

This darkening day is when he truly realizes he no longer can speed down the ice roads of bitter winter with a frozen woman in the cage of his head. This gray day is truly the time to kick away any and all the oriental or occidental horse crap in his brain, kick the damn black tar, kick it back to the strange and alien continent it came from. Hours later, after a wrecker has righted his barely harmed car, he rides bravely toward home. He has died once, been reborn, and has almost died again.

And in the soft inferno of sweet history, in the wood smoke of cognitive disruption, he bids farewell to Black Buffalo Woman and all the other red women who have night-danced around colonial campfires singing of love's true failure. "Oh, bang me in the big butt, my little pig butt frozen pizza town," he sings to them, knowing they will all meet up again soon in the great hirsute hereafter, knowing that no intruder will ever stand upon his secret grave site. Then he lights his red pipe and cries tiny dark words that are easily eradicated in the bright white light now bleaching his mother, the earth where roses—roses, they can't hurt you.

*for four Skins: Luke, Joel, Steve, and Trevino*

## *Tuba*

The dance of differing
orthographies is all
but forgotten now.
Her stomach spoke
an ancient fish language
of the *Cui ui ticutta.*
His stomach chattered
ancient squirrel words
of the *Koop ticutta.*
Now their grown kids eat
*tuba* once in a red moon
and talk only by e-mail.
He dares not boss her around
anymore—Lord, if he did, she
might inhale Jim Beam and
race to the Indian cemetery
and piss on the grave
he so foolishly keeps
crawling out of.

## Small-Town Harvest

They're all abuzz
at the post office.
The postmistress has
decided not to run for
the school board again.
*Too many people get mad.*
*Too many late phone calls . . .*
My neighbor, the widow,
enters the post office and
slams right into me before
she comes to her ancient
senses and sees who I am.
She hugs me and she's *never*
pressed her wrinkles on me.
"How's your health?" I ask.
She starts detailing all the ills
of her house: the roof's leaking,
and the pipes keep freezing up.
A huge elm limb has fallen onto
her rotting backyard fence.
"Your health, your health," I say.
"Oh, I'm fine," she says. "I did
have a heart attack last month
but I'm doing just fine now."
She shudders, squints at me.
I ask where her glasses are.
"I got in the car without them,"
she says. "Lucky I didn't run
over no people." She giggles.

I tell her of my job in Minnesota
and how I'm only able to make it back
twice a month. I've been
telling her monthly for six years
now and she still doesn't get it.
"I was wondering," she says.
"I guess I'll see you tomorrow."

She gives me yet another hug
and I leave the building and
drive east of town. Nebraska's
frosted and sloping Sand Hills
are slowly thawing to spring.
Out of the dire frozen soil
I see years rise up into
the banal sky and blend
together and I smile like
I enjoy such phenomena.

The years rise up and mix
up the memories of all
I have forgotten and that
which I can never forget.

The years rise up and shine
like my small-town brain did
when I was shy, a tittering virgin
unable to comprehend the perfidious
monkeyfuck that my American life
was and ever would be.

## Unrequited Love Among Fossils

Soap operas of the psychotic
don't happen much among
the earnest, slow elk I herd
with, so it's little wonder I
was tumescent upon leaving
the territory last week to
read my rhymes at a cow
college several hundred
flat miles from my own barn.

Afterward the congregation
adjourned to a local gin mill.
About twenty of us ancient
literary losers herded our slow
selves into a dank back room
of the local student hangout.
After a few slugs, we started
to thaw, happily squatting in
an increasingly charming Camelot.

I parked my caboose by a woman
I barely knew. She was not tenured
to torpor like me. After three drinks
(and I'd known her only vaguely
for sixty minutes) she was playing
footsies under the table with me.
Maybe a blazing blue and purple
alien meteorite alit in her glass
of single malt scotch because
for some seemingly bipolar reason

she said the most peculiar words
I heard that most peculiar night.

She said she secretly *loved me*
upon hearing my bloated verse, so
in my drunken confusion I told her
I loved *her* too, although I'd never
had *one* loving thought about her.

She told me she didn't want to hurt
her husband and, good God, I didn't
want to either—*what the hell were*
*we to do?* She suggested telling him
she and I could meet one weekend
a month at a local motel. She said
she could convince him it might be
a good idea. *Jesus, what next?* Did
I have to do him on occasion too?

I'd never even seen her husband,
though she said he wrote, but, Lord,
what if he were some kind of kung fu
academic serial killer? The meek kind
of droning professor who secretly
owned a spate of dissecting knives.

The Springsteen gargled in vitro
inside a faux antique jukebox:
"At least for a little while, sir,
me and her had us some fun."
Springsteen, never the brightest
bulb and now a fading rocker,

was warbling, and I didn't know
who the Christ I was or why
my gray-haired groin was
making me dance such
a weird fandango,
such an archaic and
undignified penis polka.
But I persevered.
Late, late, late into
the night I persevered
in the holy name of Art.

## The Indian Lit Panel

Okay, I *am* getting paid to bare
my bones here today, so when
you ask me to extemporize on
the existential inadequacies
of stolen red lives, especially
my own stolen half-red life,
I must answer sans two faces.

As much as I'd like to, I can't
just cross my eyes and blurt,
"If you know, you know—
if you don't, you blow."
Or "Hey, screw you
and the Association
of Indian Literature horse
you settlers rode in on."

But I can't spume truth either.
I can't say in my medicine
bundle I hold the ghost locks
of a handful of holy women
I lost because I worried
too much about stuffing
my face with the false
grease of fate and when
it came time to simply hold
them they slipped away.
I can't tell you of the footless
or legless guys I have known
on dialysis who begged me

to score them short dogs
of "green lizard" or weed or
worse, a hell of a lot worse.

Of course I would never
reveal how I've tottered
through the torrential spittle
of drunken chiefs and horrid
self-appointed spokesmen or
academic "Indian experts" who
named themselves "Native" but
had *never* danced poverty's circle,
and since I'd survived my own
mad sad liquid samba, they
drank me up like I was some
featherless jive angel of bent
self-love and loathing, but I still
love them and we moan together
now, hand in hand, through this
textless hologram, this hello
to historical holocaust, this
hilarious exercise in futility.

## Pu Nee'e

There, in that spirit sedan
rusting behind the tall
buckbrush, is where I
fearfully first loved myself.
Dry desert children that
we never had dance there.
Sad, wild spirits of failure
shimmer in an untamed
cliché of sunset, flaming
into the eventual invisibility
the invaders planned like
sermons of hellfire bloated
with marshmallow righteousness.

*Pu nee'e,* in the next world,
we will speak the tanned truth.

## The Last of the Saiduka

*The Paiute Indians and the long-legged redheads did not get along well. The Indians accused these giants of being cannibals and waged war against them. After a long struggle, a coalition of tribes trapped the remaining Saiduka in what is now called Lovelock Cave and set it aflame and the Saiduka were annihilated.*

STEVE McNALLEN

And if you subscribe to legends,
these Saiduka were all baked
dead with the exception of one
drooling *vata loca,* who looked
like a blend of Raggedy Ann
and the bride of Frankenstein
when she banged on my brain
door vast months ago. Sleep-
staggered, nose bleeding from
the high ammonia of morning,
I should've answered the bell,
except those winged monkeys
from *The Wizard of Oz*
were swarming over me
and one had his simian
pecker pressed against
my tired ass and I didn't
want to get pregnant
so I was fighting with all
my macho might. When
I finally broke free, I saw
her car leaving my driveway.
She tried to get me the next
day and I would've answered

but I recognized her number
on the caller ID and all I could
think of was the week before
when I drove her drunken body
home and she assumed I was hot
for her and did a staggering
striptease, lowering her slacks past
her hips all the way down to
her red pubic hairs, making
me freak and run to my car.
I could *never* bring myself to
touch pale flesh so hellishly
adorned with fiery red hair.
Red hair on the skin indicates
red worms in the brain.
*Insane in the membrane.*

Yet a couple days after that
I almost fucking relented.
For a moment (old fool
that I am) I was going
to let my heart touch hers.
My fat heart is an old cow,
an affectionate Holstein . . .
huge slobbering tongue
and glowing moon-pie eyes.
My mottled heart galumphs
into occasional fragrant fields
of sweet spring grass, blind
to the red stringiness and
the red memory eternal
of its own native flesh.
Yes, my heart occasionally
forgets its own foolish age,
but when it licked her pale
heart it sobered quite quickly.

Once I saw a turkey buzzard
dead on the side of the road.
I don't know why I stopped
my car and stared it down, but
one of its filthy, gnarled claws
still firmly grasped a chunk
of death-stink, maggoty meat.
That vile, leathery claw is
what I tasted when I licked
her Saiduka heart. I was going
to let my dark spirit touch her
but in a rare velvet moment
of blessed sanity my ancestor
spirits decided they did not
want my fat corpse just yet.
They didn't want me carted
up to a white heavenly sky
and fumbled like God did to
the great red-skinned Satan.

## Across the Wide Missouri

I cross the wide Missouri
south of Platte and an hour
later I'm lost in dry corn in
the middle of somewhere:
a small bar with a hundred
hunting rigs parked outside.
It's pheasant season, but I
need to flush out the dust.
I've never been here before
because—God—it's a titty bar.
Deep in the sticks . . . a titty bar.
After four beers I'm just another
rat in a pack of ravenous rapists.
We're pirates on a crazed ship
and all are missing an eye
or maybe a chunk of dick
which will soon miraculously
regrow atop our rib cages.
Then we'll profess camaraderie
and be titty-loving, gun-toting
American boys.

## Ruby Valley Song

*Wind rises first in the high places.*
*There is dust from the whirlwind.*
*There is dust from the whirlwind.*
*There is dust from the whirlwind,*
*the whirlwind on the mountain.*
NUMU GHOST DANCE SONG

### I

The Newe coyote tells
me about cutting willows
in Jarbridge, then going
to relatives in Owyhee,
and I tease, tell her that
real Indians only exist
downwind of Beowawe.

We laugh and talk about
how *our* cousin ancestors
boogied upon alkali, dead sage,
desiccated lizards, and danced
past the ghosts of bored wives,
grown-fat and spiteful children,
black rock, rattlesnakes, all other
imagined enemies of the soul.

*Sister, we may be Newe*
*or we may be Numu, but*
*we still talk the same walk.*

Little whirlwinds in the lives
of our ancestors removed
clutter, cleansed their very
selves, brought them back
to the center of *the people.*
God came in the voices of
laughing neighbors, in the
smells of campfires roasting
rabbits, a shared sacrament
and sadness, the sameness
of joyful differences.

**II**

Our relations were just minding
their own business when aliens
interloped in nightmare waves.
No one invited *them* in. *They*
seemed to think *they* owned
the soil, the water, the air,
all spirits, and all people.
If we didn't stick fingers in
ears, we might have heard
these creatures say *they*
owned the sky and stars.
Little whirlwinds in *their* alien
brains scattered *their* words
unto meaningless configurations
our ancestors knew as lies. These
Taibo had no shame in believing
*their* own lies. Thus, our way
of life was slowly murdered.
This is no great epiphany.
This tale is old with mold.

Every tribe in North or South
America has its own version.
It is truly nothing new and I
only repeat it because again
the Jesus people have forced
us all to forget the darkness
of their own history and I
can only mutter and curse
my own impotent awareness
of another false American war.

Grandfather, now I'm asking
how we can put a halt to being
totally digested by the monsters.
Must we suffer forever because
we were in a fog of peace when
these carnivores swarmed upon
us and smothered us with kisses
before they bit huge chunks
of flesh from our bones?
They still do that, Grandfather,
they won't stop doing that,
so I pray, I beg for you to halt
their insanity before we are
pushed into a buffalo dance
in the eternal boneyard where
our final red whirlwind swirls.

*for Francesca*

## Art Lesson

Barely past the millennium,
some fifteen-year-old
high school kid from
the state of Washington
drew a picture of an Arab
in his art class and said Arab
had the head of our born-again
president stuck atop a scimitar.
*Typical high school horseshit.*
When I was that stiff age, I was
whacking off five times a day.
A fifteen-year-old boy does
things he will be unable
to remember at thirty.
At forty he'll be incapable
of recalling that at one sweet
time he was fifteen, and surely
at fifty the thought of spurting
five times daily will seem
like pure science fiction.

His art teacher, in a goofball
and perversely patriotic act,
decided he should rat out
the kid to the Secret Service,
who then come to interrogate
this threat to the daft Moses
of the white Bible belt set.

Okay, I can accept the fact
that brown shirts seem to
hang in half this country's
church closets, but what I damn
sure *cannot* fathom is how
any "art" teacher can be so
ignorant of the holy bones
of the simple word "art."
Doesn't the word, in addition
to ancient and proscribed
attributes of instruction
and delight, also titillate
the concept of vision unto
epiphany and eventual truth?
Buckaroos, is not *art* a crawl
toward a closeness with God,
with Allah, with the Great
Mystery? If it isn't, then do
please disregard this rant
I've been spoon-feeding you.
I'll hand you your Indian
head nickel back, but give
me one moment, please—
some suave *federales* in cheap
dark suits are finger-fucking
my fearmongering doorbell.

## The Whiteheads in RVs

I take Interstate 385 north
of Chadron toward Rapid City
and stop on a deserted stretch
of road before I pee my pants.
Usually nothing is out here,
nothing but the sad backside
of dear Mother Earth, and
I can pull onto the shoulder
*anywhere* to drain the vein.

But today the road is a beehive
of whiteheads in monstrous RVs.
Bug-eyed, white-haired skulls
peer out windows, looking
for some new sights to see.
Hey, there's nothing to see
out here except my bladder
blessing the yucca plants.
*There's nothing here to see.*
There's nothing to see anywhere
in this damn solar system,
you pompous old fools. Stay
home and stare at the floor.
Wait for death with dignity.
Abandon ye your many-wheeled
and glittering 10 mpg sarcophagi.
You're the reason Arabs hate us.
You're the reason Custer got dusted.

## Paula White, the Blond Parson Woman Who Preaches Black

Increasingly, confession has become
a failed exercise in explaining
life's mysteries to myself.
This might be a good thing.
Maybe I've outgrown the art
of deception, and perhaps
creating art is no more
than saying, "I am pretty
and you are not" or "I know
God and you never will."
(*Can I get a witness?*)

Increasingly, evangelists say,
"I'm anointed and you are not—
fool, my juice squirts up into
the clouds and is welcomed
joyously and yours is not."
(*Sing hallelujah.*)

Within the confines of Now,
I'm on the couch with devil flu.
I lack strength to change CBN,
the channel of God's true voice.
*Will we hear such holy hooting*
*when we croak and zoom upstairs?*

And jeez Louise, who the holy
hell *is* this loony white woman with
her stone God Jones bone dance?
*She's pale but she's preaching black.*

It's almost like a comedy routine,
no, it's real, she's really doing this.

And I'm a person who thought
once that the strength of rap
music wasn't whether it was
good or bad but that it brought
white kids into the black fold,
making the once-white gray
matter of this nation dance
a dark détente with
the ghosts of slaves.

But this Paula Jones and her
silly simonized sermons are
truly a Golgothic mystery.
(*Praise Jesus.*)

Come on, Parson Paula.
You couldn't talk that way
unless a slew of black mambas
had not somehow slithered
into the blond Eden below
your once-bland Bible belt.
God-touched or not, Paula,
you are indeed some real,
real strange "new white meat."

## An Ode to the Eunuch Inside

A bulletin on CNN says the national threat level has been raised to yellow. My once-itinerant voice is slammed, cold caged into my once-red heart. Has the great pandemic of fear nut-punched me? Stage left: an invisible army of poets is posting poems on the Poets Against War Web site. Is this Vietnam redux? Gutlessness is not my new cri de coeur, but anymore saying anything against anyone might make the ghosts in my glands pulse my sky amber. So I behave, politely suffer the dullards I work with, and pray my annuity grows fast like cancer. Once I knew the fear of fear was the fear to fear, but these days I'm too tired to sing. Slap a yellow magnetic ribbon on my ass. I'll join the craven parade. Down, down any yellow-brick road to escape this pissoir the Dakota Indians named Minnesota.

## A Somewhat Abbreviated History of an Indian Lycanthrope

*I saw a werewolf with a Chinese menu in his hand*
*walking through the streets of Soho in the rain.*
WARREN ZEVON

When I need blood
my rotting heart
reeks and rants, clots
into such a useless lump
of mordant unhappiness
that no horizon of blue-
birds or blue erector pills
could ever sappily soothe.
I've jizzed the same jazz
forever, eternally weary
with the crushing shade
of the soil I sleep under.
I am so tired of being
a lycanthrope that I've
decided I have no choice
but to investigate myself
and seek some relief.

Don't get me wrong.
I'm not a suspect, but
I am a "person of interest."
I've left better angels of
my nature out of the loop
in deciding to put myself
under strict surveillance.

For now I'm staying
close on my tail, but
this is scary business,
rambling down streets
after my shambling self.
What the hell happened
to my posture? God, what
a lard ass I've become . . .
a cowardly old wolf
afraid to bare his neck to
any pack's culling fangs.
I am a sad longhair with
nothing to offer but tales
I tell like a sad Scheherazade
around soft campfires where
giggling deer women fry
sizzling slices of wolf flesh.
They are young and for now
take pity on my shaggy soul.
How long this will last I do not know.

## Girls Gone Wild

*One man looks at a dying bird and thinks there's nothing but unanswered pain, that death's got the final word, it's laughing at him. Another man sees that same bird, feels the glory, feels something smiling through it.*
TERRENCE MALICK, *THE THIN RED LINE*

Sometimes I lift my skull
and finger my brain and imagine
the Saudi boys finishing evening
prayers and then going out to
the nearest greasy McDonald's.
Later that night some members
of another cell are coming over
to discuss the change of heart
many of them have recently
had while living in the belly
of the disgusting infidel.
The two groups convene
in a pastel California motel
and laugh and snack on
sweet figs and plump dates.
They have almost reached
a consensus to resist
the fiery fist of jihad.
They will stay in the U.S.
They will become citizens,
hard workers, and taxpayers.
They will pledge allegiance
to the flag of the United States.
They giggle and sigh. What
a tremendous relief this all is.

They turn on the late-night
television and watch
an infomercial for
*Girls Gone Wild.*
Their eyes whirl
and spin backward.
It is as if Muhammad
has not spoken but set off
mousetraps unto their dicks.
It is then they know they
will do what they must.
They'll guide the silver birds
into eyes of such sickness.
They will blind the howling
beast-father of such harlotry.
One man looks at a silver bird
and sees not much more than
protracted boredom and wishes
science could bend time better.
The Arabs see that silver bird
and feel strange glory, feel Allah
actually smiling through its eyes.
In the soul of souls they pray
the promised martyr's reward
of a bevy of heavenly virgins
will look fine, super-sexy-fine
like those sweet-ass American
girls gone wild.

## ***Tzo Noh Hoh***

He asks if the Juneau folk hauled
me to the Shrine of St. Thérèse
where he took Townes Van Zandt
years before, and I say, "Yup."
Then he says, "Frequently now
I'm getting electricity shooting
down my goddamn left arm."
Says, "You don't hear from me,
then say me an Indian prayer."
Adds, "It don't matter, though,
because in Folsom I already
seen the crazy smile of God
on the faces of stone killers."

I say, "Yup."

*for Buddy*

## Note to a Pine Ridge Girl Who Can No Longer Read

I keep dreaming these dreams
where I lose you, literally lose
you like misplaced car keys,
and wake up sweating and
call and cuss, mutter for you
to reveal yourself, not in dream
but in my wide-awake frustration.
Thank God my closest neighbors
are simple Hmong who think all
Americans are crazed cannibals.

Ah, sweet mumbling darling,
I've been offered a great job
far from these mindless Plains
at a white castle of utmost
pay and supreme prestige.
Oh, love, what are we to do?
A decade of intense meds
has made your face puffy.
I don't look any better, but
you cannot talk—little light
breaks in your eyes when I visit.
The *wasicu* staff tells me your
*chanli* will now be cut off
because you keep putting
the lit end in your mouth.
Pain and indignity flood
our being and our memory.
I can't tell you how many times
we've sat holding hands while
you've dirtied your diapers.

Two of your toes have curled
into claws—two of your fingers
did until they chopped them off.
*God forgive me for okaying that.*

When I catch your attention
and stand before you and do
the twist, you sometimes still
smile crazily, my little one.
That you smile at my dance
of tears is enough, my love.
Dearest woman, that *is* enough.
That is *all* I need. That's plenty.
Forgive me once and again
for thinking of only myself.
Everything is clear now and
I will not be crawling away to
some new life at this late date.
I'll keep playing the game
for the paycheck and
you, my love—
eternal.

## The Ceiling Mirror of Memory

### I. Nebraska Sand Hills, 2006

Lord, because you postponed
my sautéed swim through Satan's
stew with a deft manipulation
of the CT scan, I hereby announce
the timely demise of King Louis,
the northern Nevada fuck machine.

It was a long time coming.
A long time coming, Lord, but
this new suit is ill fitting, so please
excuse any occasional lapses into
lurid urges and the irony of this bottle
of blue pills and the lame background
music of the formerly licentious Louis
warbling weird love songs into
the ceiling mirror of memory.

### II. Charles Street, Beacon Hill, 1969

A couple in a Cadillac stops in
the middle of the road and beckons
me over, me stoned and tripping
down streets of the new republic.
They offer me a hundred bucks
to come back to Brookline with
them to come with them. I am
no victorious figure of bravado
ossified young, but I am young,
so young that I'm startled to see
my smile in their rearview mirror.

I behold a long-haired tawny
Tarzan who laughs eerily
when they say they have
boodles of jungle-jazzed hemp
and good gin too, but I only
want to sniff their blood, their
ancient, ethereal Brahmin blood,
like any poor desert boy would.

## The Scorpion and the Frog

A plump, licentious frog lounged in a plastic Wal-Mart lawn chair by the fetid river. Nursing a cooler of pale ale, he watched his glow become one with the late-April sun. Then a skinny scorpion wearing a red bandanna glued to its bean sauntered up to him. The scorpion, whose yellow soul reeked of meth and rotten teeth, said, "Yo, my amphibian cousin. Listen, I need someone to ride me across Old Man River. Could you ferry me on your fine lime back?"

Irritated to have his meditation interrupted, the frog said, "Bug, you think this is *Fear Factor* or some reality shit TV? Listen, ugly, if I do that, you'll sting my ass and I will die, and I'm not ready for hell's hootenanny just yet. I don't want to drown, fool. You think FEMA or any part of the elephant regime will save my sorry democratic soul?"

"Why would I sting you? Then I'd be drowning too. Just give me a lift and I'll buy you a bottle of primo hooch," the scorpion said and smiled ever so sincerely. "Kentucky's best, Black Jack—a liter, no less. And a six-pack of Coke, Pepsi if you like, lemons, Snickers bars, whatever floats your boat."

The frog thought about it for a few greedy seconds and then decided to risk it. Besides, he had some friends he wanted to see on the other side. "So be it," he said to the bug. Halfway across the deep but placid river, he felt a sulphuric scorch in the middle of his back. The gangbanging *Euscorpius* had stung him. The frog panicked and thrashed, trying to buck the insect off. Somewhere in the pained compression of time that fear births, he screamed at the scorpion, "Christ, homes, why the hell you go and do that for?"

"Brother, my brother. What do you want me to say? *Don't fear the reaper? This is life and life only?* Clichéd as it sounds, I did it because I'm a scorpion and it's my nature to sting."

The liar laughed and was overly smug, mayhap because of drugs, this bug thug was. "It *is* my natural nature," he said, smiling at employing such a mindless phrase.

"Bitch, you've got to do better than poke me with that tiny stinger of yours," said the now fearless frog. "I've been stabbed by midgets with mightier swords than yours. And don't hand me that crap about nature. Since you refuse to dismount, I'll be forced to submerge while I contemplate such matters. But your submergence, I am afraid, will be of a much longer nature, naturally."

Underneath a smirking sun, the frog was sharpening and polishing the stinger he'd pulled from his flesh only a few weeks earlier. Now he thought of lancing his enemies, he thought of founding a new religion based upon the stinger, the stinger could be the bedrock of the new Temple of Frog, the stinger could be Wovoka himself reincarnated. He shook his glossy green head and reveled in the weight of his thickening brain. He was thirsty, oh so very thirsty. His deep dryness made him dismiss any and all dreams of true salvation. He put the stinger in his back pocket and hopped to the local pawnshop, where he hocked it for glittering coin of the realm.

A few hours later he was back at the Little Waldorf, a small, dusty bar on the outskirts of town, drinking draft beer and eating weak, greasy chili. As his eyes adjusted to the darkness, he noticed several butt-ugly scorpions shooting eight ball at the far end of the bar. He contemplated their stingers. His thoughts turned again to the Holy Order of Things, all that God stuff, that good old-time religion where angels danced the sweaty jitterbug and then stumbled off to do their dirty mischief. Love, love was thick on his frog lips when he staggered toward the scorpions. Their arachnid loins began to throb. How was the frog to know that they were waiting for payback, waiting to inject slow death into their cousin's killer?

## Nixon and Stingers

*In October 1973, American-Soviet tensions were peaking over the Arab-Israeli war, and British Prime Minister Heath's office called the White House just before 8:00 P.M. to speak with President Nixon. "Can we tell them no?" Henry Kissinger asked his assistant, Brent Scowcroft, who had told him of the urgent request. "When I talked to the president, he was loaded."*
ASSOCIATED PRESS

We're in a dump called Naomi's.
It used to be called something
else and was dank and homey
until they made it light and airy.
It serves barely adequate food
in the front; the back bar has
five televisions and a jukebox
usually thronged with hordes
of well-oiled C students from
the University of Mediocrity.
Finished with shrimp scampi
and exhausted from working
my choppers upon rubbery
and once-frozen sea critters,
I want a strong, sweet drink,
the opposite of an aperitif,
the soft rear end of linear
imbibing that is maybe a
good port, I can't decide.

After a barely adequate meal,
Pichaske orders me a stinger.

It's smooth, has several levels
of taste and kick ass, has real
nuts, actually filberts, and
is so damn good that I have
to order one more for the road.

Holm, friend and colleague, says,
"Stingers—Nixon's favorite drink."
"Really?" I ask twice and twitch.
It's a chore to recall that sane folk
hated Nixon almost as much as
liberals now hate G. W. Bush.
Nixon was a brilliant evil bastard.
Bush Jr. is a born-again goober, a
faux Elvis of the religious wrong,
so somehow really more evil.
I stagger home and Google
"Nixon and booze" and come
up with numerous references
to dry martinis ("his favorite"),
one hit on rum and Coca-Cola,
one on "Navy grog," and several
to fine wines, but nothing to
tie Tricky Dick to stingers.

Richard Milhous Nixon is dead
but his political progeny can still
sting me, so I hum "Hail to the Chief"
and don the stoutest of nightcaps
my peace-freaking cupboards contain.

## Jesus Finds His Ghost Shirt

Somewhere along the Via Dolorosa
Jesus noticed Mary was AWOL.
Further steps were uncalled for.
His carpenter's heart exploded.
An ejaculation, a quicksilver
burst of evanescence, birthed
stars so fragile that tears
seemed quite pointless.
He put down his burden
and went to his car at the curb.
Rummaging around the backseat
he found evidence that made all obvious:
a checkbook, deposits from unknown johns,
too many rolls of unopened LifeSavers,
plenty of cherry lip balm, and cheap
condoms in tawdry Day-Glo shades.
And a soft shirt of fringed deerskin
which puzzled him so deeply
that he felt compelled to put it on
and rise from the dead.

## *Bagre del Pecos*

*Estéban, como le va?*
What kind of loco BS
*were* you thinking, amigo?
Talk about sleeping
with the fishes . . .

Because I was secluded
in the great ignominy
of my necessary cave,
I didn't hear the news until
months later and I suppose
if I'd read your letters more
closely I'd have gotten a hint
but life had my groin in a vise.
My dance blinded me to yours.

*Bagre del Pecos,* I wanted to
drive over, tell *su esposa* how
sadly gut twisted I was, but I
could only send a lame e-mail:
"Sorry to hear the bad news.
If I can provide any help at all,
please do let me know."

She seemed so sweet
when you introduced us
on my last visit to Wisconsin.
I don't know what it is, man.
It might be the verse curse.
It might be the *borracho* blues.

No doubt our jalapeño blood
does not help matters much.
Your wife said in your final
dryness you returned to Aztlán,
that your ashes were scattered
in her Guadalajara graveyard.

*Bagre,* my breathless compadre,
there is no poem that matters
except the one for breath.
*Oye vato,* in our blessed finality
there are no poems at all, only
the adobe bricks we've grunted
out one by one over the years
to build sun-baked mausoleums
that will crumble like memory
in time's rusting sunset.

## E-Nebraska Main Street Cam

*Everything's gonna be all right.*
*So no, woman, no cry. No, woman, no cry.*
BOB MARLEY

My ancestors would think this
impossible or possibly evil, but
I'm in Minnesota looking live at
a small Nebraska town a few miles
from my own house of ghosts.
October 23 and it's 3:00 A.M.
Smoking a whacking cheroot, I
dance distant miles via electricity.
The Nebraska village is hazy,
almost like light snow is falling,
but I see leaves on a nearby elm.
Snow won't come until Halloween.

You're fifteen miles to the screen's left
in the nursing home in Chadron.
Our unlit house is fifteen to the right.
I am 495 miles to the northeast and
you are making the final approach
to the airport of your existence.
If there is a God, if there is
a Great Spirit, then we shall
kiss soon like we first did
in a blue terminal
of brilliant red ganja.

## The Reservation

How do you
sweep a dirt floor?
How do you describe
the blue face of death
to a spirit you will
someday dance with?
*First, a dirt floor*
*cannot be dirty.*
*Second, her face was*
*more green than blue,*
*the color of malachite*
*or a crumpled dollar*
*bill in a wino's hand.*
*We lived so red*
*in the corpse blue*
*shadow of turquoise.*

## Wabuska

### I

Stung by scorpions of poverty,
I always dumped loose change
into a mason jar until last year
when I outgrew democratic vistas
and went to Wal-Mart and bought
a five-gallon galvanized bucket.
I filled it in six slurred months
and then hobbled briskly
into the bright night rainbow
of some supermarket machine
and returned with a pail empty.
I now refuse to drop pennies
into my bucket and have
started tossing them away.
*The teenaged boy I carry*
*inside weeps at the wisdom of*
*such beautiful American waste.*

### II

*Summer 1963.* There is a shiny
propane tank on the left side
of an old railroad shack moved
onto a ten-acre plot not far
from Campbell Ranch Rez.
I lean on it from time to time
and with a small nail scratch
hieroglyphics denoting my
current worries and pain.

I scratch out the image of
a small mason jar and
the numbers 10L and
6R next to it. I date it
and draw a human foot
with a bulbous heel.
A few months later I draw
a bullet with the initials
JFK in its center and a sketch
of a cross broken in two, my
first atheistic masturbation.

**III**

*Fall 1963.* There is shiny
relief in a bell jar buried ten
steps to the left and five to
the right of the propane tank.
I want to use the money to
buy new football shoes since
the ones I have rub my heel
raw and give me a bloody limp,
but some weeks later my mom
comes home from the bar with
a purple nose and a black eye,
so the next day I go to town
and at the five-and-dime I
splurge my cash coins on
a card and bottle of cheap
perfume, Evening in Paris,
as if *I* were the guilty party.
Had I a heart then I'd have
bought a box of 12-gauge shells
for the pale flesh of my demon
stepfather, a daft zombie dancing
now through his ninth damn decade.

## IV

Because I grew up with
no running water, my life
has flowed with constant thirst
for money and the false sanity
it might purchase, but I'm still
poor forty-odd years after
the fact, and every day in this
life now I fight myself over
which raging bills to feed first.
But with my salary and this
and that and even figuring for
inflation, I do okay for a
poverty-stricken fool who prays
on late whiskey-shaded nights:
*Blessed be the poor . . . My Lord,*
*and blessed be whores like me.*

## ***E Numu Du Wi***

Dark, fat-boy clouds are
smothering snowy Sierras.
Below, an aunt, an uncle,
cousins, second cousins,
twelve Numu scrunched into
one big-ass Indian smile.
Someone has his hand
behind my head giving
me rabbit ears and surely
I have the grandest grin
in the ghostly group.

For fifty years now
dark angels have come
to my sleeping side
and have jacked me
off, trying to soothe
aboriginal sin and
my anger at being
sculpted so awkwardly
in the sadly imperfect
prefectures of poverty.
It took me a half century
to accept that I could
never be well rounded
no matter how hilariously
my half-breed hard-on tried
to slide into America, so I
learned not to smile in public.
But this photo is a perfect
image of ancient smiling.

This picture, clear and alive,
is twenty-nine years old.
Of the twelve beings, only two
still breathe Indian air. The rest
now snuggle with ancestors and
I am eternally far from home
and might cry if my aging
eyes had not transformed
into the desert of my birth.
Soon, soon, my relations,
we will all smile again,
forever together, tortured
no more by sentiments we
learned from the pallid outside.

## Ghost Dogs

Synapses short-circuited,
thoughts shoot flickering,
freezing like strobe lights
some incoming kelp,
a few whining ghost dogs,
our prairie of iridescent
evaporation, flesh dancing
from love's bones, and
memory vanishing as if
army ants were smuggling
it out the back door
of my brain.
*And I am the healthy one.*
Alzheimer's has chased you,
my love, to an unknown land,
too distant to be tracked by
the invisible bloodhounds
baying behind my dry eyes.

## Our American Life

The big green tractor
with 666 painted on the fuselage
was not so much a tractor but
an old aviator's jacket, the cracked
leather burnished with red shoe wax.
We'd pulled into a burger joint in deep snow
and ended up spinning our wheels and you
asked, "Do you want me to walk back home
for the shovel?" and I said, "No, let's sit."
You jumped in the backseat and put on
a short skirt and black nylons and said
you would get a truck to stop and help
us out. I didn't like that idea and began
rocking the old beast until we
were freed into fields of history.

## *About the Author*

A half-breed Indian, Adrian C. Louis was born and raised in Nevada and is an enrolled member of the Lovelock Paiute Tribe. From 1984 to 1998, he taught at Oglala Lakota College on the Pine Ridge Reservation of South Dakota. Prior to that, Louis edited four Native newspapers, including a stint as managing editor of the *Lakota Times* and later *Indian Country Today,* the largest Native paper in the United States. Since 1999, he has been an English professor in the Minnesota State University system.

Louis has written a dozen books of poems, the short-story collection *Wild Indians and Other Creatures,* and the novel *Skins,* which was made into a feature film. Louis has won various writing awards, among them a Pushcart Prize and fellowships from the Bush Foundation, the National Endowment for the Arts, and the Lila Wallace–Reader's Digest Fund, and was elected to the Nevada Writers Hall of Fame.